THRILLING
SCIENCE AND
TECHNOLOGY
Jobs

VIDEO GAME DESIGNERS

Ruth Owen and John Willis

AV2
www.av2books.com

Step 1
Go to www.av2books.com

Step 2
Enter this unique code

QWYLDTO5M

Step 3
Explore your interactive eBook!

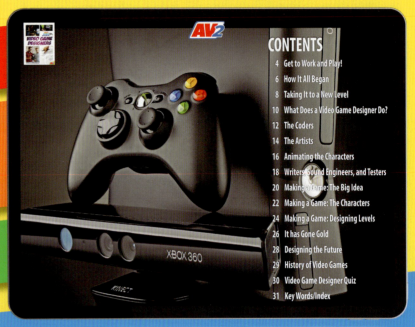

CONTENTS

AV2 is optimized for use on any device

Your interactive eBook comes with...

Contents
Browse a live contents page to easily navigate through resources

Audio
Listen to sections of the book read aloud

Videos
Watch informative video clips

Weblinks
Gain additional information for research

Try This!
Complete activities and hands-on experiments

Key Words
Study vocabulary, and complete a matching word activity

Quizzes
Test your knowledge

Slideshows
View images and captions

... and much, much more!

VIDEO GAME DESIGNERS

Contents

Get to Work and Play!

It is just one minute to midnight. In a crowded shopping mall, thousands of excited video game fans are waiting. Tonight, a new action-adventure game will be launched.

Maybe you are in the line, eager to play the new game. Or maybe you have already played it—hundreds and hundreds of times. That is because you are the designer, or developer, of this soon-to-be hit game. Sound like a cool dream for the future?

It does not have to just be a dream. The video game **industry** is a big business. This means if you love playing games and have good computer skills or lots of creativity, you might one day get to work as a video game designer.

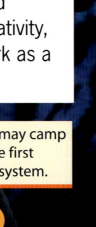

When demand is high, people may camp out overnight in order to be the first ones to get a game or gaming system.

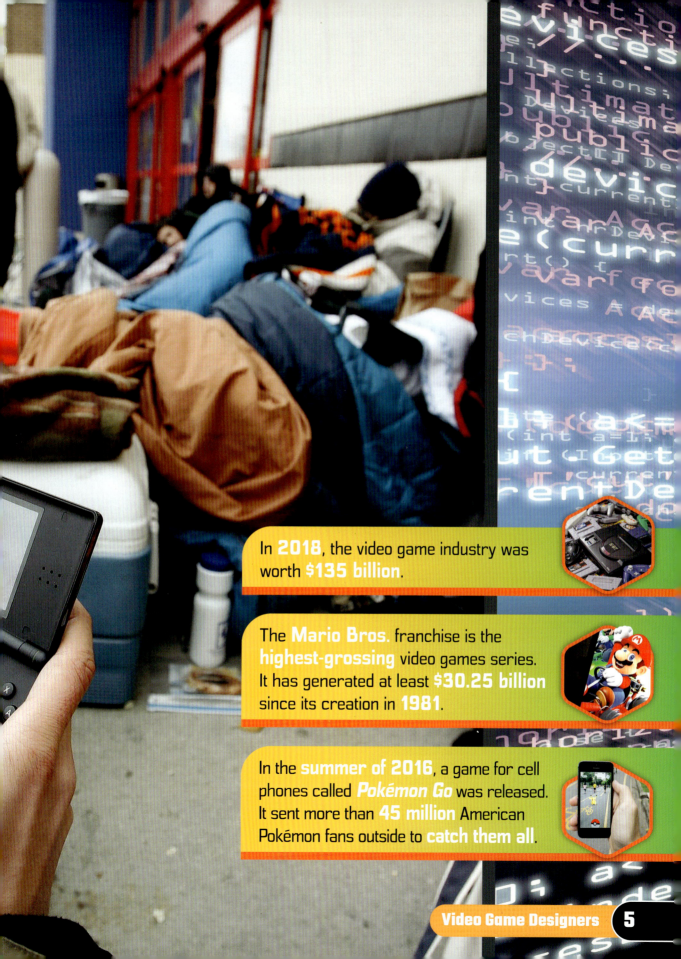

In **2018**, the video game industry was worth **$135 billion**.

The **Mario Bros.** franchise is the **highest-grossing** video games series. It has generated at least **$30.25 billion** since its creation in **1981**.

In the **summer of 2016**, a game for cell phones called *Pokémon Go* was released. It sent more than **45 million** American Pokémon fans outside to **catch them all**.

How It All Began

The first video games were created by **computer scientists** more than 60 years ago.

In those days, computers were enormous, room-sized machines. Only a small number of scientists knew how to **program** and use them.

In 1951, a British company named Ferranti built a game-playing computer called NIMROD. The computer was built for a science exhibition in London. At the exhibition, visitors got the chance to play a counting and **strategy** game against the computer. The game was called *Nim*.

NIMROD's creators did not design the game so people could have fun. They wanted to show the world that it was possible to program a computer to do math calculations.

NIMROD computer

Game display

Control panel

The NIMROD computer was 5 feet (1.5 meters) tall, 12 feet (3.7 m) wide, and 9 feet (2.7 m) deep.

The Electronic Delay Storage Automatic Calculator (EDSAC) was built by scientists at the University of Cambridge in England.

GAMING

In 1952, British computer scientist Alexander S. Douglas developed a computerized game of tic-tac-toe, called OXO. The game was played on a computer called the EDSAC. A person played OXO against the computer.

Taking It to a New Level

In 1962, a team of computer scientists at the Massachusetts Institute of Technology (MIT) designed a two-player game called *Spacewar!* As the players tried to shoot their opponent's spaceship, they had to avoid being sucked into a star. To play the game, the team built control boxes from scraps of wood and wire, along with odd bits of electrical equipment. *Spacewar!* was designed to show what a computer could do. It also showed that computer games could be a lot of fun!

Worldwide, computer scientists got to work building computers and developing games. By the 1980s, video game fans were playing games at **video arcades**. At video arcades, players enjoyed games such as *Space Invaders* and *Pac-Man*. People played some games standing at upright cabinets. Other games were played on table-like machines that had a small screen in the tabletop.

By the 1990s, games were played on home consoles and handheld devices such as the Nintendo Game Boy.

In 1982, there were 13,000 arcades in the United States.

Major Video Game Companies in the United States

Scale

250 miles

0   402 kilometers

Microsoft, Redmond, Washington

Microsoft was founded by Bill Gates and Paul Allen in 1975 and branched off into video games in 2002. Microsoft is known for its Xbox gaming system.

Sony Computer Entertainment, San Mateo, California

Sony Computer Entertainment is a branch of Sony that was founded in 1993. It has offices in the United States, Great Britain, and Japan. Sony's gaming system, the PlayStation, is one of the most popular worldwide.

Electronic Arts (EA Games), Redwood City, California

EA Games was founded in 1982 by Trip Hawkins. It has studios around the world that focus on different types of gaming and devices. EA Games is most known for sports video games, such as the FIFA series.

What Does a Video Game Designer Do?

Today, there are hundreds of thousands of video games. Whether the player is mining and crafting, matching candy shapes, or fighting mutant creatures, it is the designer who comes up with a game's idea.

The designer decides on the game's rules, the player's **objectives**, the **levels**, and the look of the game. Some games have just one designer, while others have many designers working together.

Once a designer has an idea, he or she may then work with a development team. The team will include **coders**, or programmers, artists, writers, sound engineers, and testers. Each team member has a role to play in making the designer's idea come to life.

Video game designer Jaakko Iisalo created the mobile app game *Angry Birds*. His game has now been adapted into two feature films.

A designer's idea might be an action game that plays for 10 hours or more, such as *League of Legends*, or it might be a mobile game that can be played in just five minutes, such as *Tetris*.

GAMING

It is possible for one person working alone to create a successful video game. Some games, however, are created by teams of up to 1,000 people!

The Coders

The development team members who write a video game's **code** are the coders. When you make your character run, or a door in a haunted house slowly opens and creaks, it is the game's code that makes this happen.

Coders also write the code to create a game's **artificial intelligence (AI)**. These are the parts of the game where the game must think for itself. The game's AI decides how many zombies will stagger toward you. It also decides how the groaning undead will act when you wave a flaming torch at them. An action game with realistic **three-dimensional (3D)** images may have up to 3 million lines of code!

Coders do all their work on computers using special code-writing **software**. Writing video game code is complicated and difficult. To do this job, a person needs strong computer science and math skills.

Code is the language that computers speak.

Coding Video Games

Code can be used for many tasks in video games, such as moving a worm around a square.

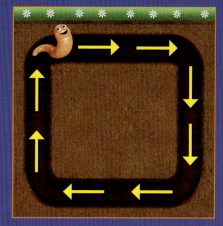

```
for (var count = 0; count < 4; count++) {
    moveForward(100);
    turnRight(90);
}
```

Coding is one of the most valuable skills in creating video games.

GAMING

Many games are built using a "game engine." Game engines are computer tools that can be used to connect the coding, art, and sounds that make up a game. The engine powers the game and helps it run, like an engine in a car.

The Artists

A video game designer imagines how a game will look. Then, a team of artists creates a world of characters and **environments** out of the designer's ideas.

Concept artists are the first artists to work on a new game. They make hundreds of rough pencil sketches, detailed colored drawings, or pieces of digital art. Their work helps the team understand how the characters, environments, and game world will look. Once the designer is happy, character artists and environment artists take over.

Character artists turn the concept artist's ideas into 2D or 3D characters. To create a 3D character, an artist makes a rough shape of the character with modeling software. Next, using shapes called polygons, the artist creates a more detailed model. Finally, the artist adds skin, fur, clothes, armor, and other details to the model.

Environment artists also use the concept artist's ideas to create a world for the game. From alien planets to abandoned cities, spooky graveyards to medieval dungeons, they create the game's backgrounds. Environment artists use modeling programs to build the game's scenery.

Sometimes, video game designers will study hundred of pictures to create scenery or creatures in their world.

GAMING

Character artists use the real world for **inspiration**. For example, they might study military uniforms to create an outfit for a soldier. A crocodile's skin might be the inspiration for the scales on a dragon.

Environment artists add colors and textures, such as rock and metal, to their models. They do this by using programs such as Photoshop.

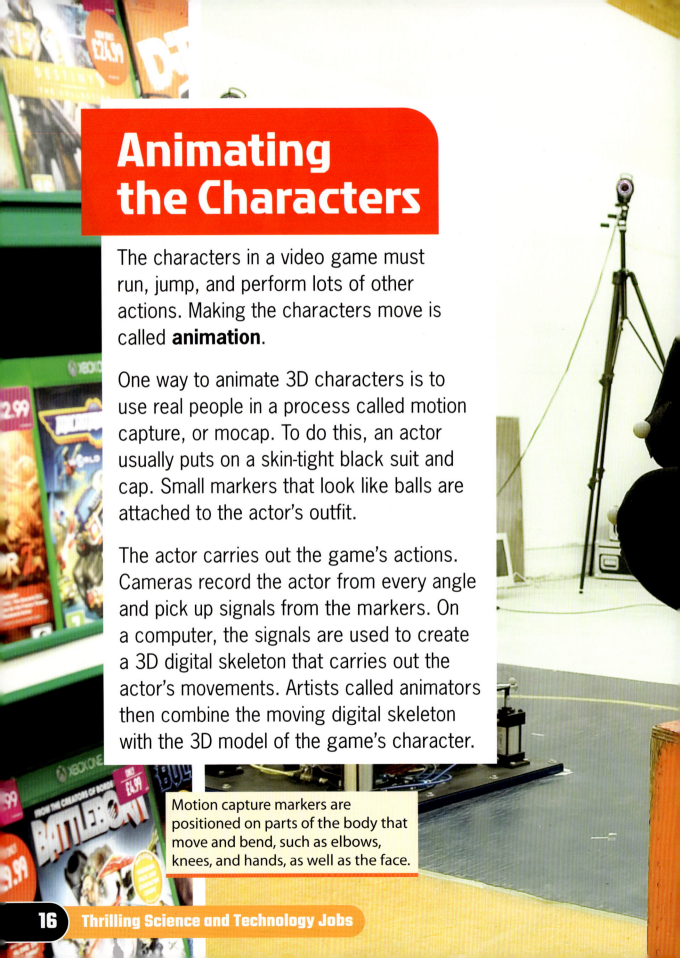

Animating the Characters

The characters in a video game must run, jump, and perform lots of other actions. Making the characters move is called **animation**.

One way to animate 3D characters is to use real people in a process called motion capture, or mocap. To do this, an actor usually puts on a skin-tight black suit and cap. Small markers that look like balls are attached to the actor's outfit.

The actor carries out the game's actions. Cameras record the actor from every angle and pick up signals from the markers. On a computer, the signals are used to create a 3D digital skeleton that carries out the actor's movements. Artists called animators then combine the moving digital skeleton with the 3D model of the game's character.

Motion capture markers are positioned on parts of the body that move and bend, such as elbows, knees, and hands, as well as the face.

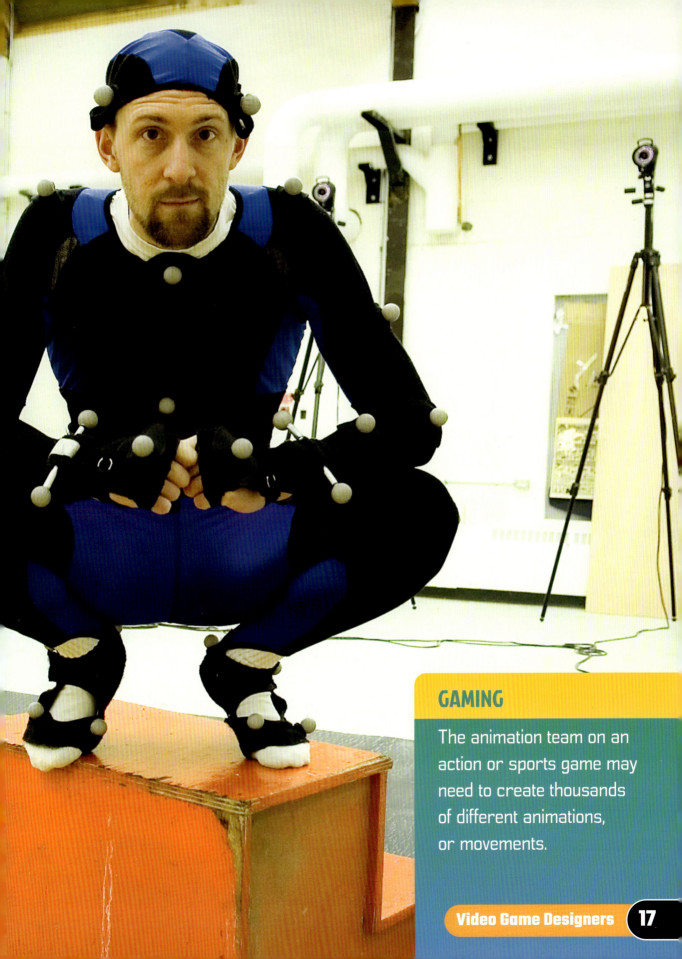

GAMING

The animation team on an action or sports game may need to create thousands of different animations, or movements.

Writers, Sound Engineers, and Testers

The other members of a video game development team may include a writer, sound engineers, and testers.

A writer helps develop a game's story. A video game designer may want to set her game in an abandoned, ruined city. The player has to move around the city and dodge mutant humans. Why is the city ruined, though? How did the people become mutants? And why are they after the player? The writer works with the designer to create this story.

Sound engineers produce the music we hear when we play games. They also create a game's **sound effects**. Sound engineers might record real sounds to use, such as footsteps crunching on glass. They also use computer programs to create sounds such as swords clashing or moaning mutants.

Before a new game can be released and sold, it must be played and tested hundreds of times. This is the work of video game testers. A tester plays a game to find bugs— parts of the game that do not work. Then, the tester reports the problems back to the coders so they can be fixed.

A sound engineer uses a mixing desk to work on the music for a video game.

GAMING

Most video game writers also develop the dialogue, or words, for the game's characters. Then, actors are recorded speaking the characters' words. The actors' voices are then added to the game.

Video game designers must create an entire world and history for a video game to make sense.

Making a Game: The Big Idea

So you want to create a video game. But where do game designers get their ideas from?

Video game designers can be inspired by watching movies and reading books or magazines. Playing board games might inspire them, too. The neighborhood where they live, a lesson at school, or their hobbies can all give them ideas.

Once they have an idea, there are hundreds of details to think about. Action, sports, driving, role-playing—there are many different **genres**, or types, to choose from. Is the game for young children or older players? Is the game educational? Is it for one player or two? Perhaps it is a massively multiplayer online role-playing game (MMORPG), such as *World of Warcraft*. In this type of game, hundreds of players from all over the world can play at the same time. Players control a character **avatar** and go on quests and solve puzzles.

Fans of online games such as *World of Warcraft* play the game at events around the world, as well as in their homes.

GDD

Once a video game designer has an idea, he or she creates a Game Design Document (GDD). A GDD is a detailed plan of everything that will be in the game.

What is in a GDD?
- The story of the game
- The gameplay
- The objectives and rules
- The levels
- The characters

GAMING

Video game designer Satoshi Tajiri created the world of *Pokémon*. As a child, Tajiri's hobby was collecting insects to study them. This hobby inspired Tajiri to create his game in which players collect *Pokémon* creatures.

Making a Game: The Characters

If a video game idea includes characters, they will need to be created. A game's characters might be humans, orcs, aliens, robots, or animals. They could also be something completely new. For example, Pac-Man is one of the best-known video game characters of all time. He is just a simple yellow circle with an eye and a big mouth.

Many video games include enemy characters. An enemy might be an evil wizard, a rotting zombie, or even an angry vegetable. You will decide how the enemy character looks and behaves. How will it attack the player? What special skills or weapons will it have?

To create a character's look and actions, a designer works with artists, animators, and coders.

A game may include tools that allow players to customize the characters. Players can choose a character's skin color, hairstyle, clothes, armor, weapons, and other gear.

Video game designers create all sorts of characters. Characters may range from cartoon animals to realistic-looking humans.

The video game character **Kirby** is named after **John Kirby.** He helped **Nintendo** win a lawsuit against **Universal Studios** in **1982.**

Only one person, a man named **Billy Mitchell**, has beaten the game *Pac-Man*.

The surface area of the *Minecraft* world is actually **9.2 million times larger** than **Earth**.

Making a Game: Designing Levels

Most video games have different levels. Each level in a game may take place in a new environment. It will challenge the player with new skills to learn, enemies to overcome, and puzzles to solve. In some repetitive games, each new level looks similar, but it is harder or faster than the last. A video game may have just 10 levels or several hundred!

A video game designer may begin work on a level by sketching it on paper. Next, the designer or coder builds a gray or white box level on a computer. This is a basic version of the level. It includes no details, but it allows the designer, coders, and testers to test play the level.

If the designer's ideas work, the level is ready to be polished. Now, the artists and coders get to work creating the final version of the level.

Video games with multiple levels can take anywhere from one to three years to create.

Some games, such as *Super Mario Bros.*, show players the level map.

GAMING

Video game designers, artists, and coders create maps of a game. A map can show the whole game world. Each level may also have its own map to show players what is to come.

It Has Gone Gold

Video game designers love creating games, but they still need to earn money from their work.

Once a designer has an idea, he or she may take it to a video game **publisher**. A publisher is a company that manufactures and sells games. If the publisher likes the idea, the company may pay the designer to produce the game. Then, the designer will bring together a team of coders, artists, and other people to work on the game.

It can take several years for a large team to produce a realistic 3D action game. Finally, after thousands of hours of work, the game will be finished. When this happens, video game development teams say a game has "gone gold"!

Game fans play new games each year at the E3 Expo in Los Angeles. This is an event where game publishers launch and show off new games.

GAMING

Some designers publish their own games and sell them online through an app store. The designer is paid a small amount of money each time someone buys and downloads a game. These types of games can sometimes be created in just a few days.

Designing the Future

The technology behind video games is developing fast. Something new is always just around the corner.

Today, some video game designers are working on games that can be played in virtual reality (VR). When a player wears a VR headset, the player feels as if he or she is actually inside the game's world. Many existing video games cannot be played with this equipment. So new virtual reality games are needed for the future.

Some video games now allow players to create their own levels and environments. Then, they can share their creations with other game fans. This means players are actually becoming designers of the games they love.

If you love playing video games, perhaps designing games will one day be your career. No one knows what the next big game will be or who will create it.

Perhaps it could be you!

It is estimated that the virtual reality market will be worth $101 billion by 2027.

History of Video Games

Video games have come a long way from their origin on giant computers. Games can now be played on laptops, stationary and portable gaming systems, and cell phones.

1972 *Pong*, a simple table tennis video game, is created.

1977–1979 Early at-home video game consoles, Atari and Intellivision, are released.

2000 Sony's PlayStation 2 is released. It is still the best-selling game system today, with more than 154 million sold.

January 31, 2000 *The Sims*, a life simulation game that allows players to create their own human and life, is released. This release has spawned three more updated versions, and is still supported today.

April 12, 2012 *Candy Crush*, a puzzle game, is released and becomes one of the most popular games in the App Store. 93 million people played at its peak popularity.

2017 Live Trivia gaming, with apps such as *HQ*, *Joyride*, and *Cashshow*, becomes a new craze.

March 3, 2017 The Nintendo Switch is released. It can change from a handheld device to a television-connected console.

2019 *Fortnite* has approximately 250 million players worldwide. It is one of the most popular games ever made.

Video Game Designer Quiz

01 What kind of game is *World of Warcraft*?

02 What does a virtual reality game make the player feel like?

03 How long can a video game with multiple levels take to create?

04 What do sound engineers do?

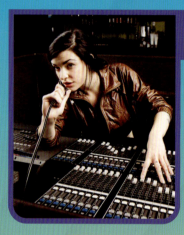

05 What do environmental artists do?

06 Which popular puzzle game was released in 2012?

07 What is the highest-grossing video game series?

08 Who is the only person who has beaten Pac-Man?

09 What is the animation process where a real person is used to accurately portray motion and emotion?

10 What was the first video game called?

ANSWER 01 MMORPG **02** They are inside the game **03** One to three years **04** Produce the music in games **05** Create the world of the game **06** *Candy Crush* **07** *Super Mario Bros.* **08** Billy Mitchell **09** Motion Capture **10** *Nim*

Key Words

animation: a technique that makes drawings, computer images, or 3D models move in a video game or movie

artificial intelligence (AI): computer programs that allow computers to act or think for themselves

avatar: an icon or character figure that represents a player in a video game

code: a language of letters, numbers, and symbols that is used to give instructions to a computer

coders: computer experts who write the code for video games

computer scientists: scientists who study and develop computer software. Computer scientists study new ways in which computers can solve problems and be useful to people.

environments: in computer games, areas, such as abandoned cities or jungles, where the gameplay takes place

genres: type of books, movies, or video games. For example, horror, science fiction, and action are all types of genres.

industry: the businesses and companies that produce and sell a particular product

inspiration: a source of ideas

levels: in video games, environments or stages that the player tries to complete

objectives: goals to reach or challenges to overcome

program: to give a sequence of instructions to a computer so it performs a particular task. Also, the word for the sequence of instructions written by a computer programmer or coder.

publisher: a company that produces and sells products such as video games, books, or magazines

software: the programs that are used to operate computers

sound effects: a sound, other than music or voices, that is artificially created for a video game, movie, or TV show

strategy: a plan of action that helps a player win a game

three-dimensional (3D): having or appearing to have height, width, and depth

video arcades: places where people can pay to play video games and other entertainment machines, such as pinball or pool

Index

Get the best of both worlds.

AV2 bridges the gap between print and digital.

The expandable resources toolbar enables quick access to content including **videos**, **audio**, **activities**, **weblinks**, **slideshows**, **quizzes**, and **key words**.

Animated videos make static images come alive.

Resource icons on each page help readers to further **explore key concepts**.

Published by AV2
350 5th Avenue, 59th Floor
New York, NY 10118
Website: www.av2books.com

Library of Congress Control Number: 2019957568

ISBN 978-1-7911-2193-8 (hardcover)
ISBN 978-1-7911-2191-4 (softcover)
ISBN 978-1-7911-2192-1 (multi-user eBook)
ISBN 978-1-7911-2194-5 (single-user eBook)

Printed in Guangzhou, China
1 2 3 4 5 6 7 8 9 0   24 23 22 21 20

032020
101319

Project Coordinator: John Willis
Designer: Terry Paulhus

Every reasonable effort has been made to trace ownership and to obtain permission to reprint copyright material. The publishers would be pleased to have any errors or omissions brought to their attention so that they may be corrected in subsequent printings.

AV2 acknowledges Alamy, Getty Images, iStock, and Shutterstock as its primary image suppliers for this title.

First published in 2017 by Ruby Tuesday Books Ltd.